T0381191

Getting
THERE
From
HERE

Copyright © 2015 Carol Walkner.

All rights reserved. No part of this book may be used or reproduced by any means, graphic, electronic, or mechanical, including photocopying, recording, taping or by any information storage retrieval system without the written permission of the publisher except in the case of brief quotations embodied in critical articles and reviews.

Balboa Press books may be ordered through booksellers or by contacting:

Balboa Press
A Division of Hay House
1663 Liberty Drive
Bloomington, IN 47403
www.balboapress.com
1 (877) 407-4847

Because of the dynamic nature of the Internet, any web addresses or links contained in this book may have changed since publication and may no longer be valid. The views expressed in this work are solely those of the author and do not necessarily reflect the views of the publisher, and the publisher hereby disclaims any responsibility for them.

Any people depicted in stock imagery provided by Thinkstock are models, and such images are being used for illustrative purposes only.
Certain stock imagery © Thinkstock.

ISBN: 978-1-5043-3141-8 (sc)
ISBN: 978-1-5043-3142-5 (e)

Library of Congress Control Number: 2015906099

Print information available on the last page.

Balboa Press rev. date: 07/13/2015

BALBOA
PRESS
A DIVISION OF HAY HOUSE

Getting THERE *From* HERE

Creative Strategies to Transform Your Business & Life

Carol Walkner

Dedication

To Jean Houston, Barbara Fuller, and the many people who have strategically transformed their lives through their participation in workshops based on this book.

Tell me, what is it you plan to do with your one wild and precious life?

—Mary Oliver, "The Summer Day"

Contents - What's In Here?
(And, what's in it for me?)

PHASE 1: THE BASICS 1

Gain clarity on who you are, what you value, and how it impacts you
How to crunch time

PHASE 2: WHO ARE WE REALLY? 21

Inner-self process, and action oriented exercises for self discovery
Find out what rocks your world, what doesn't, and everything in between
Plumb the depths of your Self, explore brain dominance

PHASE 3: AT THE CRUCIAL CROSSROADS 35

What Next? Experiential exercises and rituals to explore what's stopping you from having all that you desire
Action steps to inspire you to get out of your own way and have the business/life you imagined

PHASE 4: VISION UNITED 47

Feelings exercise to stay in the present moment
Visualizations to lock in your plan or that of a larger group
Create a Vision Collage/Dream board – the start of your new journey into transformation

Foreword

Jean Houston, PhD—world-renowned philosopher, teacher, and visionary thinker—pioneered the Human Potential Movement and established the Social Artistry Leadership Training Program. My involvement with Dr. Houston's salons and this training program laid the fertile ground for the creation of some of the processes within *Getting There … From Here*.

Barbara Fuller, MBA—entrepreneur, professional coach, and management consultant—was the immediate past president of the National Association of Women Business Owners, Central Jersey Chapter. Barbara planted the seeds for the concept and the book in 2013 when she asked me to do a strategic planning session with her incoming board of directors and committee chairwomen.

The men, women, and organizations that have participated in the workshops based on this book are what keep this amazing process blossoming. These people were ready to bloom where they were planted, and here is what some of them have to say about the process:

"These processes have changed my business life and personal life by leaps and bounds. My business has grown larger more quickly, with more consistency than ever before. This process was a turning point to creating this amazing life, which seems to be getting better." Steven K.

"The benefit to me, as a very creative person, was the ability to use my creative skill set to run my business profitably and effectively. *Getting There … From Here* is a must read." David L.

"If you are looking for a cookie-cutter business planning course, this is not for you! It's something much deeper and more unique—a chance to tap into a deeper *you* and to create and build a business that resonates." Theresa D.

"I learned a lot about myself and practical ways to use this process to enrich my life." Suzanne R.

"This book clarified my thinking and guided me to focus on those areas in my life that are of utmost importance to me and the future growth of my business. The process is outstanding." Yvonne J.

"I loved it! I learned a lot about myself and why I do and don't do certain things. It helped me set personal and business goals. I highly recommend *Getting There … From Here* to anyone." Patty M.

"This right-brain process helped me identify what is most important to me in both my business and my life in general. It has allowed me to take charge of priorities and conquer my day with maximum efficiency. I would highly encourage anyone that is looking for an outside-the-box approach to business planning to read this book. It will change your life!" Christopher A.

Acknowledgments

You would not be holding this book—possibly searching for glasses and wondering about it—without a few very special people who acted as fertile-ground breakers and seed planters. There are also those who have helped make it blossom and others who continue to help *me* bloom wherever *I* might be planted.

Dr. Jean Houston's Social Artistry leadership model which she used in her work with the United Nations, her numerous salons, and her other offerings provided the fertile ground that helped me to be ready to plant my seeds of creativity. Thank you, Jean, for being a mentor to me for the past thirty years. Thank you also for creating the valuable Social Artistry training, which led to the deepening of my own work and my personal transformation. Without Dr. Houston, her brilliant work, and her vast mentoring skills, there would be no beginning to this wonderful work, nowhere to plant the seeds from which this book bloomed.

Barbara Fuller, MBA was a speaker, mentor, and "cheerleader with army boots" who has provided programs to educate, inspire, and motivate young people to be business owners. Barbara asked me in the spring of 2013 to develop a strategic planning meeting for her incoming board of the NAWBO–CJ. Thank you, Barbara, for having faith in me to create something magical for your group. Without Barbara Fuller, there would have been no seeds to help this Social Artistry book project blossom. Although Barbara knew of this dedication, my heart breaks knowing that she has passed before seeing the actual book in print.

Linda Fabe, MEd—Licensed Professional Clinical Counselor, long-time friend, business whisperer, and confidant who listens deeply with a loving ear—I thank you from the bottom of my heart for always being there for me, no matter what.

My dearest son, Ryan Gorney, is ever my cheerleader, my technical support and computer guru extraordinaire, who always makes me believe, "You can do it, Mom!"

Jan Vander Linden, my best friend forever, helps me more than she could ever imagine all the time, above and beyond this book.

My best friend forever and ever, Joy Luczynski, who also happens to be my sister, is another constant cheerleader and is the one who said, "Contact Balboa Press, *now*!"

Ann Merli—my business partner in many creative endeavors, close friend, and fellow seed planter—always asks me, "What else is possible?"

Without all the courageous people who heard the call to adventure and stepped up into their own lives to participate in the workshops based on this book, knowing it was time for transformation, there would be no book and no reason for me to continue. With a heart overflowing with gratitude, I say thank you!

Preface

What is *Getting There … From Here* All About?

Getting There … From Here is about considering what else is possible for your life, for your business, and for yourself. It's about developing out-of-the-box ways of thinking in order to make all that you do a true reflection of both your values and your unique vision. If the term *creative planning strategies* seems like an oxymoron to you, you're right. You'll discover how planning and creativity merge to become transformative.

Are you a solo entrepreneur or part of a larger organization that is ready to go to the next level? Perhaps you're a frazzled stay-at-home mom of three, a person who is going through a divorce, someone who just retired, or an employee who was just downsized. Maybe you're someone trying to figure out what to do next with your life. Whatever your situation, do you have a sense that something is not quite right—that this is neither the business nor the life you dreamed it would be? Are you at a crossroads, scratching your head, wondering what's next? Are you part of a group exploring your individual and group relationships or wanting to create a more team-conscious atmosphere? Maybe your company is at a crossroads, and it's time to step up your game. Are you a non-profit wondering how to get from where you are to where you desire to be?

You will find this combination book-and-workbook valuable in finding answers for any of these scenarios.

What About Me … Me … Me … the One Reading This Book?

Getting There … From Here is about you, you, you—your business and your life—today, over the next twelve to twenty-four months, and beyond. Imagine that you're going on a trip; you know where you want to end up, but you really have no idea how you're going to get there. You have no GPS or map. What kind of trip will that be? If you're at a crossroads in your life, either as a solo entrepreneur or as part of a large corporation, it's a good idea to have a strategically guided plan to keep you pointed in the right direction and to get you to your final destination. Whether your destination is the pot of gold at the end of the rainbow or to further your own journey on a road less traveled, your time is now.

Getting There … From Here provides a profound, intriguing way to plan, to strategize, and to develop a direction that you may not have previously thought possible. You might even enjoy the ride. You can create, use your intuition and imagination, delve into yourself, and come up with the wisdom that is buried there. Insights may evolve, leading you in possible new directions. You are an explorer using an experiential, visual approach as you clarify the larger picture for your life, your business, yourself. You are developing an action plan to create your vision.

If you have wanted to put a strategic plan into place but have no idea where to start, this book was designed for you. If you are a right-brained type and the idea of a strategic plan makes you want to poke your eye out with the nearest sharp object or run away screaming, then *Getting There … From Here* could be for you. If you are a left-brained type and you have taken your team or company on a detailed journey to deeply analyze your structure, to develop mission and vision statements, and to establish goals, then *Getting There … From Here* will help you to harness your creativity and turn it into a plan of action.

It's time to make your life and your business a reflection of your values, your voice, and your unique vision. It's time to listen to your heart speak and to discover what else is possible.

Social Artistry—Laying the Creative Fertile Ground

What is Social Artistry, why is it here and how does it apply to you?

Dr. Jean Houston has been a role model and mentor to me for over thirty years. My participation in her Social Artistry Leadership Training program provided depth and evolution for my ongoing inner-self work. As part of the leadership training to be a social artist, I discovered what truly motivates me, what I value and how I might expand myself as an individual.

Trained social artists are the type of leaders who will be able to facilitate change within our very complex world. They must be wise, compassionate and courageous as they step out into a world filled with poverty, disease, inequality in class, race and gender, as well as educational and environmental issues. They will help to create populations capable of generating their own creative ideas and enacting them—thus creating the change we would all like to see in the world. There are social artists throughout the world facilitating these changes and making a difference for men, women and children in a myriad of countries and communities.

As a social artist, I have chosen to work with the people around me each day. I want to interact with you. This book, in part, is based on the concepts I learned in the social artistry training to help you develop a deeper, fuller life and to affect your individual or business transformation.

As a writer, an agent for change, and an experienced right-brained entrepreneur, I want to provide you with creative strategies and processes that will make both your business and your life journey clearer, easier, simpler, and more joyful.

Are you ready to transform your life, your business, yourself?

Synchronistic Next Steps—Blessed Be the Seedlings

When this book was just a seed that had been planted in the far reaches of my mind, I facilitated a half-day process for the central Jersey chapter of the National Association of Women Business Owners (NAWBO–CJ). A diverse group of women comprised their incoming board of directors. I created an intense strategic-planning meeting that not only established a team atmosphere but also examined individual and organizational values. The experiential exercises were fun and enlightening, and they helped the board to establish goals for the coming year. It worked for the group as a whole and for the individual members of the board. We accomplished what they had intended for the meeting, and we did it all in four hours.

As a result of that meeting, the seed that would become this book had been fertilized and was growing. Starting with the outline for that day, I began to construct *Getting There … From Here*.

Since that day, I have held many workshops based on the theories explained in this book for a variety of business people of all ages, types, and genders, guiding them through a four-phase process. No matter where the participants were in their business or personal lives, the process worked. No matter which road they were on or what they were looking for, every person exceeded their own expectations. Some of their testimonials can be found in the foreword.

Getting There … From Here has helped all kinds of people who find themselves at a crossroads to discover the best path, road, or highway for their individual needs and for their businesses. As a result, they are living the life that they dreamed of having.

The Difference Between Right-Brained and Left-Brained Thinkers

Although different, right- and left-brained thinkers bring equally important gifts and talents to the planning process. Here are the simple, basic differences:

Left Brain: logical, verbal, analytical, detail oriented, structured, sequentially oriented

Right Brain: nonlinear, creative, emotional, intuitive, big-picture oriented, visual

By approaching the planning process in a right-brained manner, you are exploring possibilities, seeing creative options, and allowing yourself to dream big while connecting emotionally with your vision. If you are doing this as a group or a team, each person's values will be part of the equation, as each person becomes part of the solution. The logical, analytical, left-brained people are necessary to keep the process moving in a forward direction. Each way of thinking is necessary and important as long as the initial vision is authentic and enough time is allowed to plug in the details where they naturally belong.

Spontaneous Writing—Uh-oh! I Am Not a Writer!

For this experience, you do not have to be a writer. (If you are, you are not going to be penalized–no worries.) Spontaneous-writing-prompt exercises will appear throughout this book, and I want to alert you ahead of time so that you do not panic when the time comes. You do not have to be a writer to benefit from these exercises. For some people, writing is like public speaking—that is, death seems easier. It's important to remember that this isn't school and that there are no grades. Remember to breathe. Don't get stressed out over the process. Hopefully as you become involved in the process, you'll begin to de-stress.

When you answer a prompt quickly and dive right in without over thinking it, you will be amazed at what emerges. You will be bypassing that left-brained critic lurking inside that tells you that whatever you are doing is not good enough, not correct, and not acceptable. Writing from the right-brained side directly connects you to your emotions and your heart. Authenticity and what is really true for you slips out. It's not scary, and it works.

The final part of the process is the invitation to share with others all, part, or none of what you have written. If you are doing this as a part of a team or group effort, the sharing can be very enlightening—sometimes even magical—as creative thoughts emerge and a deeper level of bonding happens.

How Can I Get the Most Out of *Getting There … From Here?*

Since this book is based on a creative, intuitive way of thinking and doing, there will be exercises to complete, meditations to allow you to go deeper into your own mind and heart, spontaneous writing prompts, and a vision-collage project at the end to help solidify all the work you have done. (Note to left brainers: You will survive and enjoy this! Others have. And you might even thrive.) Throughout the process, use the space provided not only to complete the various exercises but also to record your thoughts, plans, strategies, and visions.

I strongly suggest that you work through the phases in order. I understand that you right brainers get bored more easily and might not want to go in order. Keep in mind that each phase builds upon the one before it. There is also some left-brained analysis, planning, and sequencing that helps the entire process work.

When you gain clarity about yourself and your values in PHASE 1, you will be able to slide more easily into PHASE 2, where you will discover more about yourself and what rocks your world. You will explore the basis for the business you do and, for the life you are living and want to live. If an organization, team, or group is doing this together, it will become clear how the individuals' values interface with those of the organization or company as a whole.

As you progress into PHASE 3, you will be at a crucial juncture, wondering what's next. In this phase you'll further explore the life you desire and how to attain it. PHASE 4 is your action strategy. Visualizations, feelings exercises, and a vision collage/dream board complete the process to lock in your plan and acknowledge your transformational vision.

Group Notes: If you are doing this book/workbook as a group, additional explanations will be provided to assist in this process. Or, if someone decides to facilitate this process for a team the intention is for this to be clear, simple and easy to utilize for you and your team members.

PHASE 1: THE BASICS

Utilizing action oriented exercises, you will delve deeper into who you are and what you value. You'll gain more clarity and learn a time crunching meditation for use in all aspects of your business and life.

Why is it important for me to do this *now?* What is my intention for creating a strategy for my business/life?

Group Notes: Each person should state his or her name and why it is important for him or her to be here at this time. What are his or her personal intentions for the process?

Note: Monitor the process; do not allow someone to monopolize the time. Also, make sure that each group or team member knows that you are creating a safe and confidential space. What is said and done in the group stays there. This is *very important*!

State *your* intentions here (or in your notebook) now:

Values

What you value and who you are directly influences the manner in which you do business, the clients you attract, and the success of the endeavor you are in currently. What do you want most in life? Does the business you are in align with your values, with how you perceive the world, and with what you would want the world to be within the next one to three years? Do you know where you are going? Do you know how you're going to get there?

The following exercises will give you the insights to begin to answer these questions. As you dig deeper into yourself, as you age, and as your wisdom grows, your basic values and who you are as a human being will probably not change, but the emphasis on certain values might shift.

Group Notes: Sharing throughout this process is a good thing and is often magical in the safe, confidential space you have created. The exercises below will give fresh insights for the individual and will help everyone to discover who that person is and the role they play within the group. *Short group discussions should be encouraged. Sharing is invited and optional—not mandatory.*

Clustering, or Mind Mapping, is a right-brained, nonthreatening way to quickly reveal your thoughts on a specific topic. It is simple and involves just placing what comes to mind around the main thought bubble without a lot of thinking. The less thought, the more honest the answers tend to be. For this specific "I Am" exercise, the kinds of things you want to include are your qualities, characteristics, and values—descriptions and adjectives for what makes *you* uniquely you. Incorporate anything that will give yourself and the world a clearer picture of who you are. See the example here:

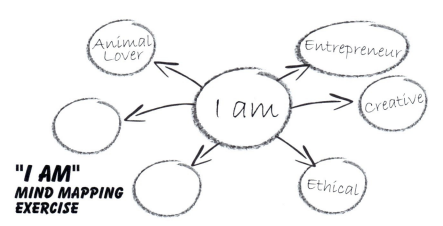

"I AM"
MIND MAPPING
EXERCISE

I Am

What Am I Really All About?

Thoughts about the "I Am" exercise—surprises, gleanings, and things learned.

Notes to Self:

What do I want most in life? If nothing pops up or if your brain is overcrowded, make a list of two to five things; choose the main one, and write a little about that.

Where am I going in business/life, and how will I get there? (This process will help clarify that.) Answer in twenty-five words or less. Don't over think this portion, and don't worry if nothing comes forth.

I know what I stand for, which is …

Continuation of What Am I Really All About

Imagine that you are your own brand manager, the CEO of Me, Inc.

What makes your business unique? If you are using this workbook to improve your life as a whole, what makes you unique right now?

If you are part of a team, group, department, company, association what unique qualities do *you* bring to the whole?

Inspiring Thoughts & Important Notes:

The Core of Me

In the following exercise, give each area some thought, and as always, give it your best shot. There is no right or wrong answer and no judgment—just hunting for deeper insight. Write what initially comes to mind, and think about additional details and reasons why you chose what you did.

If I were a car, what kind would I be? What about this car represents me as a person? (Example 1: A Jeep, because I am reliable and confident, and I can do many things without getting stuck. Example 2: A little red sports car, because I am outgoing, sleek, and sexy.)

If I were a store—any store—which one would I be and why? (Example 1: A Target store, because I am very versatile. Example 2: A high end specialty food store, because I love to cook and quality is important to me.)

If I were a restaurant, which one would I be, and why? (Example: an upscale, fun place with excellent food and good prices. I chose this because the quality is reliable, people enjoy being there, and the food is creative.)

If I were an animal, what kind would I be? What characteristics of this animal represent me? (Example: A dog, because I am loyal, a good friend, and playful.)

Group Notes: It's time for discussion, which is a great, unique, and fun way to get to know other group/team/department members. Go for it! No judgments or comparisons. You can share just the last four prompts, or you can include the "I Am" exercise as well.

Did you notice any key insights? Were you surprised by any of your choices?

More About the Core of Me

What is most important to me at my core? What drives me?

When I feel as though nothing could be better, these are the values I am exhibiting:

When I've felt conflicted in the past, this is what was happening in my business/life:

When my values were not honored, this was the situation:

Here is what lights me up, what I am passionate about, what I feel strongly about, what drives and excites me. (Lists can always be a good place to start if the words don't seem to come freely. Lists of three are most productive.):

This is what turns me off, dims me down, or bores me to tears:

This is who/what seems to be in control of my dimmer switch. Who, what, why, and how? If I'm not in control of this part of my business/life, what's up with that?

My Most Important Core Values

(A value is an important quality at the deepest level—meaningful, worthy, and deeply true. An example might be kindness.) List your values, writing quickly whatever comes to mind, without a lot of deep thought. When you write this way, you are bypassing your natural critic and judge, and allowing what's in your heart to flow out. Keep writing as long as the words, thoughts, ideas keep coming. If you feel stuck, you can approach this from the viewpoint of what bothers or irks you in other people. For example, if someone is not being kind to another and this bothers you, then kindness could be something you value. If your list is long, narrow it down to the top three that resonate the highest for you. If you have only one ot two, that's good enough.

Enhancing the Senses—Using All of Them in New and Creative Ways

In the beginning of this process, as we delve deeper into ourselves, it is important to awaken our senses, which activate our capacity to think, feel, and understand things in multiple ways. We can appreciate more deeply the world within us and about us. And in the process, we become more sensitive to those around us.

As we become tuned to our five senses of seeing, hearing, tasting, smelling, and touching, we also become more aware of our other two senses. These are our sixth sense, which is intuition, and our seventh sense, which is, in my opinion, our sense of humor.

The following exercise enhances the senses internally, which allows you to think more creatively and see current or old challenges with a fresh eye. You can use this at any time throughout your day at work or in your personal time. You can concentrate on one sense alone if that seems appropriate to capture that fresh perspective. This was one of the exercises that I learned in my Social Artistry training with Dr. Houston.

Playing with the Senses

We are all surrounded by a layer of energy. Imagine that layer around you. To actually feel it, rub your hands together vigorously and then pull them apart slightly. You should be able to feel a ball of energy between your two hands. Pull apart a little more. You may feel a tingling sensation or a sense of a slight resistance between your two palms.

Bring your hands in front of your eyes without actually touching them, and with the energy from your hands, gently massage your physical eyes. You are also enhancing and sharpening your inner vision.

Next hold your hands about half an inch from your ears, and with your energy fingers, activate your ability to listen on many levels so that you can hear and listen deeply, with your heart and soul as well as your ears.

Now imagine yourself breathing in deeply through your nose, clearing your airways so that the air of inspiration can be taken in deeply, clearly. Breathe in deeply, knowing that air is also the vital life force and that, with each breath, creative life is being taken in. Your mind is expanding with each breath.

Open your mouth and place your fingers about an inch from your tongue. Imagine your energy fingers activating your sense of taste, as if there are teeny tiny chefs in each taste bud. Use the enhanced taste buds to help savor your inner knowing. Imagine your tongue is an instrument of expression and communication. Actually tap gently on your tongue as if tapping into a computer—your own bio computer. You are tapping in new ways of communicating and knowing. You are expressing yourself more authentically and from a deeper heart space.

Group Notes: This exercise is perfect for a group. Sit or stand in a circle and do the exercise in that form. Invite discussion afterward. Suggest that the members of the group continue to practice this on their own or together in meetings in the future.

Suggestion:

To further embody all of your senses and to get used to being more aware of them, go outside and see, hear, taste, smell, and touch your natural surroundings for the next couple of days. This even works in a city where Mother Nature may not be close. (In the work environment or home office, sit quietly in your area/office and allow your senses to take over. What do you see, hear, smell, touch, and taste within this place that is such a large part of your life?)

Remember: When you find yourself in a difficult or challenging situation, you can truly hear what is being said behind the words when you focus on and tune into all of your internal and external senses.

Inspiring Thoughts & Important Notes:

Time-Crunching Meditation

If you are used to meditating—that is, going to a place of calm and quiet—that's great. If you have never meditated before, no worries. It's easy, and it doesn't have to be perfect.

To put the senses to work for you immediately, we're going on a trip within your mind to a time or an incident in your life when you experienced considerable joy. You can be on a vacation trip that was totally fun, joy filled, and wonderful or you can go to another incredible incident beyond compare.

Use all of your senses and imagination to live in that time of joy, as if you were still there. Stay in that place for the entire time, bringing it to life again with all your senses. What did that experience look like and feel like? What smells and tastes did you experience? What did you hear during that time?

We're only going to be in that place for *two minutes*, but it will seem like a lot longer. We are learning to crunch time as well as enhance our sensory perceptions. If you are doing this as a group, either you can delegate one person as a timekeeper or whoever is facilitating can keep the time. If you are doing this on your own, set a timer for two minutes after you get comfortable before beginning your "journey."

Sit comfortably with your feet flat on the floor. Your eyes can be opened or closed (closed helps you relax more quickly). Breathe deeply through your nose and exhale deeply through your mouth. Do this four times, relaxing more into your chair with each breath.

Now imagine that time of joy—that experience that is a highlight in your life. Bring all your senses into this experience, and be there in a very deep way. Stay in this place for two minutes. You may be amazed how long a minute seems.

Inspiring Thoughts & Important Notes:

More About Time Crunching

You have just experienced a new way to look at time. You can take these same minutes to review a project, to visualize the completion of a task from beginning to end, to gain clarity about next steps, or to go from being overwhelmed and out of time to having all the time you need to complete all you need to do. Time now can become your friend instead of the enemy you thought it was.

Inspiring Thoughts & Important Notes:

Clustering, or Mind Mapping, is a right-brained, nonthreatening way to quickly reveal your thoughts on a specific topic. It is simple and involves just placing what comes to mind around the main thought bubble without a lot of thinking. The less thought, the more honest the answers tend to be. (This is the same as the "I Am" exercise on page 4.)

My Business/Life Now

Our lives, both personal and business, are a journey. We have answered a call at some point to start or be involved in certain businesses, to have friends, to have romantic relationships, to get married, to have children, to get divorced, to care for elderly parents, etc. Whatever has gone on in our lives, we have answered a call at some point, making an agreement to begin a certain journey.

If you are a reader of fiction, nonfiction, or biographies, all of the main characters, the protagonists, and the other characters around them have all answered a call. You have answered a call to be a part of a specific journey. Authors typically use this format when they plot their books, set up the story, and create the characters within that story. This is the hero's journey.

The journey you are on right now is about strategically planning the next phase of your business, your life, or perhaps both. And you are the hero or heroine of this journey. You've also answered the call to be part of this group.

Get ready for the next phase of your journey.

Homework: This is optional and very enlightening. Do some, none, or all; the choice is yours.

1. Add to your I Am statement if more things occur to you.
2. Flush out some more details about your core values.
3. Be in your own life, both business and personal, with all of your senses. Are you responding differently? Use all the senses as you go through your day. Generally be more aware.

PHASE 2: WHO ARE WE REALLY?

Explore your dominant way of thinking and how it impacts your relationships. Using, inner-self discovery processes, and experiential exercises, you will find out what rocks your world, what doesn't, and everything in between

Brain Dominance: What Is Your Dominant Way of Thinking?

Left-brained individuals are analytical, articulate, and to the point. They like identifying details and are more logical than intuitive. Left-brained people have good communication and persuasion skills.

Right-brained individuals are intuitive, imaginative, and creative. They are flexible and are concerned with the bigger picture rather than the details. They are impulsive and spontaneous, and they do not like time limits. They have difficulty explaining ideas verbally and prefer illustrations to verbal instructions.

Brain Dominance Quiz: The following series of questions will assist in determining which side of the brain is dominant for you. If your score is equal, you could be whole brained, which means you have the qualities of and operate from both sides of the brain in business and in your interactions with others. (If you desire additional information or a different test, search the Internet; it's loaded with options.) Indicate *true* or *false* for each of the sixteen statements listed below. The answer key will indicate whether a statement is more L/left-brained or R/right-brained. Compare your *true* answers with the numbered statements. If you have more L/left-brained as *true* for you, then you are more left-brained. If you have more R/right-brained as *true* for you, then you are more right-brained.

1. When going to an appointment, I am usually late.

2. When I talk, I gesture with my hands.

3. I am good at guessing time correctly.

4. When I buy something new, I like to read all the instructions before using it.

5. I daydream often.

6. It is easier for me to remember names than faces.

7. I turn my head to the left when someone asks me a question.

8. I like to organize my time and set goals for myself.

9. When I listen to music or a favorite radio station, I work better.

10. People ask me frequently if I am listening to them.

11. When in conversation, I concentrate on what is being said rather than how it is said.

12. When making an important decision, I analyze all the pros and cons.

13. One sign of a genius is a messy desk.

14. If I have much to do, I begin with the easiest tasks first.

15. I write my holiday greeting cards early.

16. When I begin a new task, I relate it to one already accomplished.

Answer Key: 1.R, 2.R, 3.L, 4.L, 5.R, 6.L, 7.R, 8.L, 9.R, 10.R, 11.L, 12.L, 13.R, 14.L, 15.L, 16.R

Right- or Left-Brain Dominance: Knowing how people think will give you more clarity about why you click with certain people and why others rub you the wrong way. If you are observant, you can tell what type of person you are dealing with by noticing how he or she dresses and how his or her house or car is kept. From a business perspective, when you call on someone or go into his or her office, the following are some important observations to make.

Is the desk neat with any visible papers (there won't be many) aligned? Is the person sitting up straight with all clothes starched and professional? Are all writing utensils in place? There may be a pen set displayed in front that might have been an award from long ago. The chairs might be lined up, the books arranged carefully on shelves, the credenza dust free and clear on top. If there are family photos, one or two will be carefully placed on the desk or credenza behind the desk. This person is left-brain dominant.

Is the desk piled with stacks of papers, some possibly toppling to the floor? There might be newspapers, magazines, and other business publications scattered around. If there is a credenza, it is piled with more papers, books, articles, and accoutrements of the business this person is in. Photos will be all over the room. The person's clothes may be rumpled; they will be professional but put together with some imagination. Men's ties may be askew or they may wear no tie. Women may wear scarves and dress with a touch of flamboyance. This person is more right-brain dominant.

Idea: Look at the people in your life—business and personal—and see if you can tell if they are left- or right-brained. Then communicate with them according to *their* style. Does it change how you are with that person or how they are with you? Play with this.

Right-, Left-, or Whole-Brained—Everyone Has Inner Experts

We're going to delve deeper into ourselves and take a look at the inner "expert." That expert part of you is the experienced, knowledgeable, informed part. It's what you are really good at, the area in which you are very skilled or highly trained. Get to know better all the roles you play within your lives, and learn how these roles might be helpful in moving your business forward in the best way possible. What are your skills? Are you skilled in music, painting, knitting, swimming, fishing, cooking, golfing, teaching, or creating? What are you really good at?

There are many roles you might play—business person, husband/wife, father/mother, brother/sister, friend, mentor, golfer, computer whiz, etc. Your skills, various roles, and relationships impact all that you do, including your business. You have within you inner experts that you can draw upon as needed to help move you and your business forward in a positive direction.

Important: As you think about your skills, roles, and inner experts, *imagine* how you will use these skills and inner experts to make a positive impact on your business.

Writing Exercise

To better access the right side of your brain, you are going to do a writing exercise. You *do not* have to be a writer to do this. In fact sometimes it's better if you're not.

Sharing your completed writing is invited, and you always have the option to pass or share only a few lines.

You can also share it all; it's up to you. Sharing helps other group members more than you may realize. If you are doing this on your own and have a trusted friend, spouse, or colleague, you may want to share some of this with that person. As always, it is your choice, but you never know from where additional insights might come.

Write quickly without worrying about spelling, punctuation, etc. Just write whatever comes to mind without judgments. It will be like stream-of-consciousness writing. This type of writing bypasses your left-brained critic, who judges everything you do, so that you can get to the heart of the matter.

Choose *one* of the prompts below and write for about ten minutes. If nothing pops into your mind, start with a list of skills or strengths.

Writing Prompts: For now choose only *one*. You can always write more later. This is a right-brain exercise, so freewheeling, stream-of-consciousness writing is a good thing.

1. I am skilled at or have a lot of expertise, knowledge, and experience in _____ (list at least three). How do these skills/areas of expertise impact my business?

2. My three main strengths are _____. In what way do these strengths impact my life and, potentially, my business?

3. I look at my business/life through the eyes of the expert part of me. In what ways does it look different?

Room to Write More:

Group Notes: This writing prompt is perfect for team building and for bringing additional cohesion to a department or group of co-workers. Sharing is typically magical, as people within the groups often realize how united they are in their thinking *or* find themselves more open to hearing alternate ideas and new thoughts in the vulnerability of the sharing.

Inspiring Thoughts & Important Notes:

Retracing Your Steps and Adding Anew:

Go back to the "My Business/Life Now" mind map/clustering page from Phase 1 (page 19). What might you have added during the time between sessions? And might you be looking at it differently right now after the skills/expert/strengths writing exercise? How so? Perhaps there are more concepts or ideas to add. If so, do that now.

Food for Thought: Are your skills, strengths, and areas of expertise being utilized in the most appropriate way? Are they being used to your best advantage in your business? What about in your life? Is there a part of the business that is outside of your skill set, or is there just "stuff" you don't like to do that you might delegate to someone else? It's time to think outside the box—maybe way outside the box.

If you are part of a larger group process or company, are there tasks or projects that might be reassigned to others more suited to the completion of that project or task? Are you consistently doing things that you really dislike doing in a business or your life? Is there a better or different way to do them? Think about it. Imagine it.

Have a quick group-brainstorming discussion about the possibilities of delegating. The rules of brainstorming are that there are no rules, except that you may not judge what *you* think or what anyone else says. Throw even something farfetched out on the table. Who knows how you might build upon it. Take eight to ten minutes. Go!

Inspiring Thoughts & Important Notes:

Review the Exercise Involving What Lights You Up and What Turns You Off:

Take a deeper look at how these aspects relate to your business/life and the direction and success, or lack of, within that business/life.

Inspiring Thoughts & Important Notes:

The guidelines are the same as before. Choose **one** of the prompts below and write for about ten minutes. (If you need more time, take it, especially if something important is revealing itself.)

Writing Prompts:

1. I am passionate about/absolutely love to do …

    (If many things come to mind, list three, and then expand on the primary one. This can be anything.)

2. My primary or most important core value is _____. This is how I incorporate it into my business/ life …

3. My primary passion and my most important core value are integral parts of my business/life, and here is how …

Room to Write More:

Time-Crunching Meditation

Use the basics of the *joy/vacation trip* meditation, but instead of a time of joy or favorite vacation, visualize the *ideal/best company, business, or organization* that you have ever been involved in. Immerse yourself in the "feelings" and the aspects of that place, even if it was your own. What made it the best? Use your five senses like you did when you went on your other trip as you visualize this company/organization. Breathe and relax.

We're only going to be in that place for two minutes, but it will seem like a lot longer. If you are doing this as a group, either you can delegate one person as a timekeeper or whoever is facilitating can keep the time. If you are doing this on your own, set a timer for two minutes after you get comfortable and begin your "journey."

Sit comfortably with your feet flat on the floor. Your eyes can be opened or closed (closed helps you relax more quickly). Breathe deeply through your nose, and exhale deeply through your mouth. Do this four times, relaxing more into your chair with each breath.

Inspiring Thoughts & Important Notes:

Another "Mind Mapping/Clustering" exercise for *your* ideal business/life. Draw a circle around the concept below and add whatever comes to mind that needs to be part of your ideal, your dream.

My Ideal Business/Life

Homework: The Executive Summary of My Ideal Business/Life

Describe your business/life in detail using the five senses. Add your sixth sense—your intuition. Now this is not a typical "head trip," describing what you think it's supposed to look like. What does it really look and *feel* like from your heart, from your intuition? Use this space for your summary.

More...

Now add your seventh sense—your sense of humor. Have fun with it. Remember the joy that you experienced from your first meditation. Pull that feeling back out, and write some more from that place of joy. How might you add this to how you do business or how you orchestrate your own life? How might you add joy to your everyday comings and goings? Your business/life is all about you. *Be the joy within that business/life.*

Inspiring Thoughts & Important Notes:

PHASE 3: AT THE CRUCIAL CROSSROADS

Exercises and rituals are provided to motivate and inspire as you ask the question what's next and explore what's stopping you from having the business/life that you imagined. There are action steps to assist you in getting out of your own way so that you can have all that you deserve

What Is Next for Me?

and

What More Is Possible?

Group Notes: Have a short check-in about the prior session, PHASE 2, and the seven senses as part of your ideal business/life.

You are ready! You are on the threshold of creating the business/life of your dreams. You have designed what the ideal business/life looks like and could be. The next phase of anyone's journey is to deal with the obstacles—both those from outside of yourself and from within—that prevent you from actually having the ideal business/life.

What is stopping you from having it exactly the way you want it? What might be holding you back from having your business/life more like you want it to be—moving in a positive direction, dynamic, and powerful? It's time to ask what more is possible.

Inspiring Thoughts & Important Notes:

Writing Prompts: Write quickly to engage the right side of the brain while bypassing the inner critic and judge. Keep asking what else is possible, what more is possible.

Here is one thing I am personally ready to do to turn my business/life into my ideal or something that works better for me. (This could be a tiny step):

The two to three main things stopping me from having my ideal business/life are:

What are the two to three areas/aspects stopping my business from becoming a stronger, more alive, more authentic entity? This could be from a business or a personal aspect. Perhaps there is a way of thinking or acting personally that is preventing you and your business from being more in line with how you want it to be, more authentic for you. If something isn't working, can you change it? What might that look like?

What two to three old habits or outdated ways of thinking or doing might I release so that I can step into my own true power and have my business/life be more authentic?

Moving forward, what two to three things might I do differently within my business or on a personal level that I have not done before that would make my business/life more dynamic, more authentic, and more viable for me? What would make it work better?

Take the *top answer* from each of the previous questions and list them here:

Passions, Personal Purpose & Core Values:

Review quickly what you wrote about. As you grow and alter your business/life, it is important to incorporate those aspects that bring you passion and more aliveness. It is essential to know how you want to feel all the time. Incorporate any additional thoughts that might have come up during the most recent exercises.

New-Life Meditation

Use the basics of the *joy/vacation trip* meditation, but instead of a time of joy or favorite vacation, you are going to imagine that it's a year from now and that you are reviewing the past twelve months, celebrating the wonderful things that happened—the many business successes that you experienced and the many life enhancements you had. You have released what is no longer serving you, and you have created a more powerful, purposeful, valuable business/life that fills you with joy. You have said *yes* to your passion, to your purpose, and to yourself.

You can actually see your business/life as the ideal that you envisioned. Immerse yourself in the feelings and aspects of this future. Use your five senses, as you did in the previous visualizations. Breathe and relax.

You're only going to be in that meditative space for two minutes, but it will seem like a lot longer. We are crunching time as well as enhancing your sensory perceptions. If you are doing this as a group, either you can delegate one person as a timekeeper or whoever is facilitating can keep the time. If you're doing this on your own, set a timer for two minutes after you get comfortable and begin your "journey."

Sit comfortably with your feet flat on the floor. Your eyes can be opened or closed (closed helps you relax more quickly). Breathe deeply through your nose, and exhale deeply through your mouth. Do this four times, relaxing more into your chair with each breath. Then relive and review your year of wonder.

Inspiring Thoughts & Important Notes:

It's All New

You have celebrated the business/life you will experience as you saw it one year from today. Write the details of this business/life using all the senses. What did your celebration look, feel, sound, smell, and taste like? What aspects of the future successful business speak to you the loudest? What is your intuition telling you to do? What more is possible? What feelings and what emotions are coming up right now?

Thinking positively, how does this new way of doing business or new way of being make you feel? When you envision the *new* in the future what are the top *positive* feelings that arise?

Choose at least two to three. (If your brain just went numb, check the Internet for a list of feelings. *The Desire Map,* by Danielle LaPorte also lists 150 top feelings on pages 72-74, and it's an extremely powerful book besides.)

Inspiring Thoughts & Important Notes:

On a scale of one to ten (one being the lowest and ten the highest) how ready are you to achieve your business/life as you visualize it?

My readiness factor is _____.

If you are at a six or below, what is holding you back from a full commitment at this time?

What might be some of the challenges to getting to 100 percent commitment?

What can you do to break down these challenges to get there?

What action steps might you take now?

Write quickly to see what might emerge.

Have a discussion about commitment. Brainstorm ideas for actions or steps necessary to arrive at the level that you would like.

Write a positive declaration statement about your commitment to your business/life. Make sure it comes from that most powerful part of you.

(Example: I will stop procrastinating, stick more closely to the plan that involves my ideal business vision, and begin taking the necessary actions or steps now.)

Homework: Keep imagining and visualizing all the aspects of your ideal business/life.

Know that you are making a difference in your own business, in your own life, and out in the world at large. This portion is always optional *and* can lead to deeper insights.

Suggested Writing Prompts:

1. This is how I make a difference in my own life …
2. These are the ways I use what I am passionate about to continue to grow my business …
3. Being of value out in the world is important to me, and this is how I accomplish this…
4. I follow my own muse and write what emerges…

When the group meets again, it would be interesting to share (optional) pieces of the homework. Sharing is oftentimes very valuable for the individual and for the group.

PHASE 4: VISION UNITED

Examine the importance of feelings and how you can stay in the present moment. Create an actual vision collage to lock in your plan for the life/business of your dreams and as a dynamic representation of your transformation. Be careful what you wish for—this dream board process can by truly magical

If you are reading and doing this on your own, do a self-check-in about how the process as a whole is going for you so far. If you are doing this as a group, now is a good time for a quick review and check-in from the group.

Inspiring Thoughts & Important Notes:

This last session is about how you want to *feel* going forward in your business/life and how those core feelings that you desire translate into your intentions for that business/life.

After identifying these feelings, you will create the *vision* that is *united* with who you are, with your values, and with how you want to feel in your business/life. If you are doing this as part of a group, your group/team/company vision will be united with your group mission and values. The values of each member within the whole are an integral part of the company vision, mission, and value system. And how each person feels within the group environment is a key to success.

Your heart and your soul will be integral parts of this vision of your livelihood and of how you will operate your life. Everything we do is driven by a desire to feel a certain way.

Feelings are power. They are how you perceive life, and perception forms how you live.

It is best that your feelings come from inside you, from something that you own. For example, instead of saying "I want to feel loved," say "I want to feel love." This puts the feelings in your own arena of responsibility, not someone else's.

Writing Prompt:

My top-ten core, desired feelings are …

(Helpful hint to generate these words: ask yourself, "What do I want to do, want to experience, or want to have in order to feel this particular way?")

Write quickly. Turn the left side of your brain off, and let your creative side turn on. Come up with at least ten feelings.

Once you have your list of words, try to determine where in your body you feel them? Can you even feel them? Take a few minutes to get in touch with your physical body and see where these *feelings* reside. Stay in touch with those feelings.

(There is a difference between a feeling and an emotion. *Feelings* are fluid, direct, energetic responses to an experience. They are communications from your body. *Emotions* are feelings with an added mental component—our back stories, our beliefs, and the patterns from which we interpret our feelings.)

Inspiring Thoughts and Important Notes:

Group Notes: Take a few moments individually to review where your feelings reside in your physical body. Discuss as it seems appropriate. Insights could abound.

It is natural to start criticizing and judging how you feel and what you want from business/life. Please do yourself a favor and *don't do that!* Keep remembering that you are worthy of your desires.

How deep are these feelings for you? Look up the words if that helps.

Caring about and knowing how you feel—how you *really* feel—on a moment-to-moment basis produces clarity. This is where the joy is, the flexibility, the peace and calm, the balance. It's where the good ideas come from, and knowing how you feel in the moment helps you to stay in the moment rather than slipping back into the past or sliding out into the future.

Go back to your joy/vacation meditation and remember how you felt during that time.

Living in your deepest desired feelings can revolutionize your life.

More Writing

Choose three to seven of the core feelings that resonate the most, those that feel the strongest to you. Have a minimum of three. List them, and then write more about them. You could use all your senses to delve deeper into these feelings.

Vision will help fulfill your desires. This is less about goal setting and more about discovering your intentions in that deepest, heart-and-soul part of you, in that heartfelt-feeling part of you.

Vision Collage Process

This visioning process is totally in your hands. You are the creator, the visionary, the imagineer for your business/life. Allow at least forty-five minutes to one and a half hours for this process. Whether you are doing this by yourself or in a group, you can always add additional images later.

You are creating a visual for your business/life, a physical representation that you can look at every day to inspire, motivate, and assist you in your own visualization process.

Materials Needed for This Process:

A photo of yourself

Poster board- Comes in white or various colors (size 22" x 24", whole or cut in half)

Scissors

Glue sticks

Magazines, cards, and old calendars from which to cut images, as well as any other image sources you might have that appeal to you.

Group instructions follow on the next page. The steps below are for individuals doing this process on their own:

Choose a color of poster board that appeals to you. What are you attracted to? Don't put a lot of thought into it. You could even start with white.

Trace your hand on the poster board. Place your photo somewhere on the board as well.

Now look at your list of top desired feelings for your business/life and choose images that will make you feel this way. The images should represent what you want your business and/or life as a whole to look like, feel like, sound like, taste like, smell like, and be like. They should come from the deepest part of who you are. The images will reflect your values, reflect who you are, and reflect what you want to experience.

Don't fill up the entire board. Leave room for the infinite possibilities that might arise later, now that you are setting your intentions and declaring your vision with *feeling*. This applies to individuals and groups as well.

Individual Life Vision Board

Group Process Directions for the Visioning Process: Make sure you have a piece of foam core that is large enough that the entire group may participate on that one board. The stiffer and thicker base material will last longer, and it allows for easier display. Have every participant bring a photo of themselves. People can bring in their own magazines, while some magazines can be provided for the purpose of finding images for placement on the board.

In the center of the board, write the name of the company and the vision you are working toward.

The group should gather in a circle around a large table, and the blank board should be placed in the center of the table.

Have each member of the group put his or her hand on the large board and trace that hand. The participants' photos should go inside or near the outlines of their respective hands. Everyone should be respectful of their neighbor's space, but they should not be reticent. Each person should have an equal amount of space on the board.

Participants should select images from the magazines that represent the way they visualize what the group is hoping to accomplish. The participants' visions will be placed together to create one vision that is united.

After the board is in place, each member of the group should speak for a few minutes about their portion of the board, about their experience with this process, and about how they envision the company/organization/group going forward as a whole.

Write about anything that might have surprised, excited, motivated, or invigorated you.

Inspiring Thoughts & Important Notes:

Group Vision Board for Non-Profit Organization

REIKI WAY
LEARNING
CENTER

VISIONING SUCCESS

Conclusion

Wow! What just happened? I was *here* in my life, and now I am *there*, where I wanted to be.

It's your business/life. You are the visionary; whether right-brained, left-brained, or whole-brained, you are the designer. You are the hero/heroine of your own bright future, and you are the one with the answers. You now have a clear idea of what more is possible. Write your own conclusions below:

The Beginning

Appendix

The vision-collage/dream-board process is an extremely dynamic, experiential exercise that could change your life. Be careful what you wish for; it could come true. The following are some stories from people who have gone through the process and are still shaking their heads in wonderment, exclaiming, "*Wow!* It's amazing how quickly …"

Arlene, who was a disbeliever and who thought herself totally uncreative, said she would come because she was my friend and wanted to help me, but she said she would not participate. Four hours later, she had a huge collage with her life designed for the entire year. In the lower left-hand corner was a scene from Disneyworld, which confused her because, although she loved that as a vacation spot, she did not see herself affording it in the near future. Four months later, Arlene got married for the second time. Her new mother-in-law gave her tickets for an all-expenses-paid trip to Disneyworld as a wedding gift.

Derek was excited to do a vision collage. He is a young man who is building his business, and he had great plans for his immediate future. One of the images he selected to include in his collage was of a man standing on a stage, behind a podium, speaking to thousands of people. His eyes almost popped out of his head as he exclaimed, "There is no way that this is me or could even be me anytime soon! The thought of speaking to a large crowd like that? Forget it! I have no idea why I chose this." Derek's business began to skyrocket, and seven months later he was invited to the company's national convention to talk about how he had accomplished such business excellence. You guessed it—he was up on stage, behind a podium, in front of three thousand people talking animatedly about his venture! (He was also confident and smiling broadly.)

My own dream-board story is one of instant wish fulfillment (although it actually took ten minutes). As a writer and poet, I had been sending out work for a long time, getting published sporadically. My specific vision collage was about getting published and being successful. A few minutes after I pasted my last image on the board, my cell phone rang. It was the State Woman's Club competition chairperson calling to tell me that I had won second place for a short story and first place for a poem that I had submitted for the state competition. The poem went on to win first place in the national competition.

Be careful what you wish for and what you place on your vision collage/dream board!

The prompts in this book, designed for fast, spontaneous writing, are based on the idea that when someone writes quickly to a prompt, the judgmental, more critical left side of the brain is bypassed, allowing the creative, right side to come streaming in. My opinion is that this creative side is connected to the heart and that the words that arise are truer and more authentic. Having been facilitating these types of writing groups for the past twelve years, I know firsthand that this is definitely how it works. When people within a group share what they have written, the process becomes magical.

Inspiring Thoughts & Important Notes:

Inspiring Thoughts & Important Notes:

Inspiring Thoughts & Important Notes:

Printed in the United States
By Bookmasters